The Hello Culture

The Hello Culture

Strengthen Customer Loyalty by
Empowering Your Employees to Be Remarkable

Joseph Taricani

To order additional copies of this book, contact:
Xlibris Corporation
1-888-795-4274
www.Xlibris.com
Orders@Xlibris.com
77368

Contents

Contents

Acknowledgement

For all my friends and former co-workers in Fort Worth, TX without whom this book would not have been written

Hello is Simple and Powerful

Hello.

If every one of your employees greeted your customers with a sincere "hello" your business would border on becoming a world-class service provider. Do you believe that? It's true. There is no replacement for quality products and services that are competitively priced, but the people of your organization can make you the gold standard in your industry. All it takes is for everyone in your business to say "hello" to your guests, customers or clients.

It is a remarkably simple principle. If you're in the service or retail industry, all your employees should make your customers, clients or patients feel welcomed, especially when they come to visit your place of business. That's the focus of The Hello Culture. When your customers come to visit you in person, your organization has an opportunity to differentiate itself. If your employees do this you'll find your customers will feel better about your business and your employees will feel empowered to make a difference. When you follow the principle to all its natural extensions you'll also discover some other remarkable changes in your business. You will begin to build a culture that is structured around making customers happy to do business with you. Your business can accomplish all of this after you provide your staff with the skill set needed to create a friendly and approachable culture—all starting with "hello."

Even before the "texting" and "posting" revolution took center stage, people were already avoiding interpersonal communications. Voicemail was a great method to avoid actually speaking with someone. Email followed and it enabled the behavior. Talking to people in person has degenerated and avoiding live interaction has accelerated by virtue of technology. Now people don't give much thought to ignoring one another. It's more culturally acceptable. Good sales people, however, know the value of a smile and a handshake. It communicates sincerity and it builds trust. The rest of us just need to be reminded that acknowledging people and talking with them is very powerful.

Sometimes really simple things are also really clever. The concept of saying "hello" may seem rather trite, but it has an alchemistic effect when knit together with some other things outlined in this book. Post-it™ notes are a good example something really simple that is both clever and profitable. An engineer at 3M Corporation set out to make strong glue in 1968. His glue was actually quite weak therefore it was deemed a failure. A few years later a fellow engineer used the weak glue to hold bookmarks in his hymnal at church. In 1980, 3M actually started marketing Post-it™ notes and now Post-it™ notes and related products generate in excess of $1 billion of revenue annually. Post-it™ notes, after all, are just little pieces of paper with some glue. It's quite common not to realize the intrinsic power of ideas or concepts. It's even more common to dismiss ideas because they don't seem very novel. Some companies understand all this very well and you'll read about them and their success later in the book. For now, however, let all this flow into you and you'll see how you can make remarkable changes in your business. This approach to customer service is indeed simple, which means it will also be much easier to train and motivate your workforce to follow you on this journey. Its simplicity also makes it rather inexpensive to implement. The clever part comes when you see the remarkable results that emanate from the Hello Culture.

For some reason we business professionals fail to apply the same standards of etiquette to our work environment as we do in our home. Imagine you invite a friend to your house for dinner and your friend brings a friend. Could you imagine not talking to that person the entire evening? You wouldn't think of it. But that's exactly what we do every day in business. We invite our customers to our "house" and we miss the opportunity to make them feel welcomed and valued. If you're a retail establishment, you practically beg your customers to come to your store but when they arrive, they're often dismissed or ignored. Personal, friendly service is one of the last weapons local hardware stores have over larger competitors like Home Depot. It also puts into vogue something we've all chuckled at—the greeters at Wal-Mart. Sam Walton seemed to understand that making you feel welcomed upon entering his store was very effective. If you're a service business, say a law firm, your client is in your office for a reason. Sitting in your lobby, the client may be anxious about their matter or they may be nervous about the fees they're going to incur. No matter what their circumstance may be, it stands to reason your client is probably a little uptight. One thing you know for sure, your client wants to be able to trust you and your firm. There is no better opportunity to enhance that trust than when they are sitting on an island in your lobby feeling slightly out of place. You should save the obligatory bottle of water and encourage your staff, no matter who it may be, to walk up to the client and make them feel welcome. Under any set of circumstances, it's always good if your customer leaves your business feeling inspired by your staff. If your customer likes and remembers the way they are treated, they will have more confidence in your business.

Like any initiative, success or failure rests with the leadership of your organization. If leaders don't embrace and spearhead cultural initiatives, they will fall short, fizzle, or fail. A half-committed leader could quickly be reduced to a cartoon strip.

Boss: I want our people to be friendlier to our customers.

Worker: . . . . *taking diligent notes* . . . .

Boss: I'm launching a new initiative and beginning today all our people will say hello to our customers.

Worker: Our biggest customer will be here in an hour, would you like to come say hello?

Boss: I launched another initiative on delegation last week so you can say hello for me.

Cartoon strips aside, every good leader will tell you they have to be fully committed for an extended period of time before the workforce develops an unconscious competence for a behavior. Although we haven't explored this yet, you should not underestimate this as a cultural revolution for your business, thus The Hello Culture. The Hello Culture gets your organization fully invested into an identity that every employee can understand. That's why this cultural journey is so terrific. It presents a simple theme that has tremendous benefits. Early on, you should expect that some of your staff will walk around and mockingly say "hello" in a dismissive tone. Some will chalk this up as silly and another reason why management doesn't deserve their salary. Later on in the book, I will explain how your burgeoning culture will naturally handle cynical employees. If you promote and sell the program like the boss in the comic strip, however, you'll surely get that response. That's precisely why you shouldn't make a proclamation. The best way to kick off the program is with a simple challenge put in the form of a question. You may ask it any number of ways, but here's what I would ask: Could our customer go on a self-guided tour of our facility and would that customer be made to feel welcomed by everyone they encountered? Or you could ask it a different way: How would our customer feel about us if they took a self-guided tour of our business and were warmly greeted along the way? The customer would notice, appreciate and remember the genuine attention. It is not an indictment on your business if you can't pull it off. Our business community has been pushed into a results-driven culture that has lost the focus and desire to engage customers. Your journey into creating The Hello Culture in your business can be self-guided, which is why the only barrier to entry is your commitment.

Here's the way to make it happen—

Every Employee Can Do it and Every Customer Will Notice The Difference

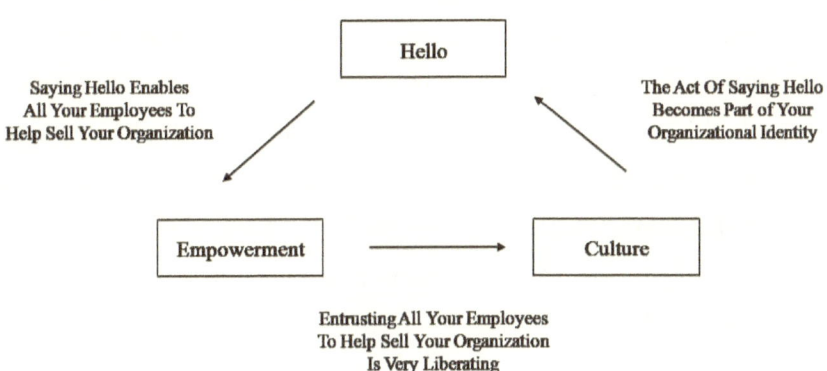

The journey from saying "hello" to creating a new, exciting culture for your business is very real. Asking employees to master a technique that has been taught to them since childhood is like giving a test where everyone will score 100%. The least experienced people in your business will perform as well as your top employees and everyone will feel the value of being remarkable. The rally cry around The Hello Culture empowers employees to make customers feel special. Everyone likes being on a winning team and everyone likes to know they can contribute to the betterment of the organization. In a short time, the culture of your organization will center on getting excited about making customers happy.

The Fine Art of Saying Hello

The Hello Culture follows a basic premise: if all your employees are willing to say hello to a customer, many of your employees will do a lot more. Some people will introduce themselves while others will probe the customer to get them talking. In other words, the average greeting to a customer, client or guest will far surpass that of any of your competitors. It's not so simple to assume that all your employees will say "hello." There could be many reasons that an employee will look away from or fail to engage customers. The employee could be having a bad day. They might lack self-confidence. They might be too busy. They might not want to interrupt if you are showing a customer around. Saying "hello" may be an act that is outside their comfort zone which merits a great deal of discussion later on. These are all things to keep in mind, but if your employees are deputized and empowered to speak with your customer, then some of them will probably react differently right away. Others, actually the majority, will give every indication of playing the role very well, but in their moment of truth they will falter.

It's important at the outset of any organized training program promoting The Hello Culture to make sure your staff understands you will not be teaching them anything new. If you walk into a one or two hour training program and tell your audience they're here to learn about the importance of saying "hello," they'll quickly tune you out. Your organization needs to see the impact of not saying hello. They need to see the downside of a customer feeling lost, nervous or frustrated. It's an easy role play. Everyone has fun recounting their most frustrating moments as a customer. If your employee is not willing to say hello to your customer, they're less inclined to be very friendly or helpful. If it's perfectly okay for your employees to not acknowledge your customers, then you're sending a message that your customers are not very important or welcomed. On the other hand, if all your employees create a welcoming experience, you've taken an important step in becoming a service provider for life.

You need patience for the employees who lack self-confidence. Shakespeare said, "All the world's a stage." If this is true, and I believe it is, you'll be asking many of your people to perform an unnatural act on an unfamiliar stage. Probably unlike you, most of your employees don't possess the natural ability to walk up to a stranger and act as a representative of the company. This is true even if you are only asking the employee to say hello. An employee that lacks self-confidence just needs a little coaching and a lot of reinforcement. Watch the expression on this employee's face when they say hello to your customer for the first time then look to you for reinforcement. It's as though they just stepped out of the bleachers onto the playing field. They have immediately gone from spectator to participant and they feel great. An employee will feel more fully engaged when they realize they have just helped solidify a customer relationship using their nascent sales skills. Employee engagement and management commitment is really the secret sauce to The Hello Culture. In this case, you have just invited the employee to act on stage with you. They see themselves as able to play at your level in some small way.

Some employees have bad days. Many of these same people seem to have many bad days. It almost makes you wonder why they are in your organization. These people have found safe haven in your business because they know they can be cranky as long as they do their job. An employee that is truly having a bad day deserves a pass. In many cases it would break your heart to know what is troubling them, so it's good to practice one of the *Seven Habits of Highly Effective People* which is, "seek to understand, then be understood." Many people, however, wear an attitude that sends off an unfriendly greeting. People's body language can easily send a message that says, "I'm not willing to speak with you." Your organization needs to learn the importance of body language. In most cases your employee can choose whether or not they want to be welcoming. This is an important part of migrating to The Hello Culture. Your people need to know that the safe harbor for cranky employees is closing for business. Let's also not jump to the assumption that your people need to fake their way into an attitude that is unnatural. Just as many employees will ignore guests, others may try to make up for their insecurities by going overboard with their welcome. Your Hello Culture needs to evolve and be natural to be sustainable. People that can't make the turn will be obvious over time and you'll determine ways to deal with them. On the flip side, The Hello Culture will start to work its way into your hiring practices. Your recruiters will start to look for people who have an affinity for genuine communications because it's an important part of your culture.

The vast majority of the people reading this book will find themselves in a common conundrum. You are racing against a deadline and you come upon a customer or guest who needs a moment of your time. Your heart is racing and you feel the anxiety of this moment's deadline, but now you're challenged with taking a pit stop in the middle of a tight race. You can do it. You've probably practiced this skill in your personal life. You encounter a person who you don't have much time for, but you also need or want to make the person feel good about your exchange. What have you done in the past? You manage the conversation, but not by starting out with a disclaimer that you only have a minute. You do so by giving a warm greeting, then you take control. You might redirect the person to someone else, you might excuse yourself to use the restroom or you may politely say there is a room full of people waiting for you. Some good retailers give their employees the proxy to drop what they are doing and walk the person to their destination. While this dilemma may or may not present itself to you, it will surely be something many of your staff will ask about. If you're in a service business this really won't manifest itself as a real issue. At best it's a red herring. You have to remember that the standard you are trying to achieve is that you want everyone to say hello. You're not asking everyone in the business to openly probe the customer for information about their childhood.

Start Your Own Revolution

You'll probably have three observations as you begin your journey into and build The Hello Culture in your business. Your first observation (maybe you've already had this one) is that this will be fairly easy. You're seeing the big picture being presented here and the dots are probably beginning to connect for you, otherwise you would have stopped reading before you finished the back cover. While none of us would ever see ourselves like the boss in the comic strip mentioned earlier, you're probably thinking that this is actually something we could pull off without too much effort or investment. In the grand scheme of training or transformation programs, the effort and investment to build your Hello Culture is indeed low. In other words, your initial observation is correct. You want your organization to warmly greet your guests and you don't have to teach a complicated theory to pull it off.

The second "aha" you will have is when you get into your program and you realize that you can't turn this on like a light switch. You'll begin noticing a lot of people who continue to walk around and not acknowledge the customer with whom you happen to be walking. You'll probably think that this person or that person has just not taken your training class yet. In reality, you're seeing that it takes a long time to burn this into your organization. You have to reinforce the behavior to encourage many of your people to act on the same stage with you. We'll talk about some reinforcement techniques later but you need to be prepared for the notion that getting your organization to say hello is not simple.

The third observation is the best one. It's the one that hits you when you realize you have arrived. There will be little signs before big ones, but you will absolutely know you are winning. You'll hear customers tell you that your people are terrific. You'll see customers leaving your business ready to commit to more business and ready to give you the benefit of the doubt if something is amiss. One customer told me once that he felt like a rock star during his visit.

The two things at the top of my litmus test are remarkable and they qualify as the best compliments you can receive in business. The first of these happens the day that your customer wants to send their employees to your business to learn from you. General Electric mastered this long ago. An invitation to GE's training facility in Crotenville gave customers the opportunity to peek into one of the most remarkable business machines in the world. Disney figured it out 20 or so years ago when they founded the Disney Institute. Every year thousands of business leaders travel to Florida to learn the fine art of paying attention to and delighting their guests. Your business can achieve that status too, and all you have to do is to get your people to say hello to your customers. The highest compliment you can receive is when your customers begin asking you how you've built such an amazing culture. It means they respect you, they admire you and most of all they trust you. You create a natural barrier with all your competitors when your customers think about you in these terms.

The other thing I look for comes in the form of remarkable compliments. A customer who owned their own business once said to me, "I wish our employees would treat our customers the way your employees treated me." Let's stop here. Great moments in history merit some reflection. Think about that compliment. That customer wasn't talking about you, they were talking about your employees. All the employees that came in contact with that customer during that visit had the effect of lifting our business to a new level. How would you feel if one of your customers came to you and said that? In my estimation it was the most profound compliment I have ever heard about a business. Within that compliment there are many messages, but the one I like the best is that the customer was inspired by meeting our staff.

If customers are inspired by meeting your staff, then your staff was remarkable. You've entered a whole new world if your staff starts to see themselves as being remarkable. You might want to think about this as a business objective. How do you think your employees would respond if you established a business objective around the goal of having customers admire all your employees? It's a very complete and fulfilling goal. It's something that people can visualize and it transcends itself into every interaction your employees have with customers. There are only a handful of companies in America that even try to claim that their employees are remarkable. Four Seasons Hotels is one of them. Four Seasons makes a basic, binary assessment of a prospective employee. Either the candidate has a natural tendency toward a service orientation or they don't. Four Seasons does not want to have to train someone to be friendly. As a result, all the employees at Four Seasons have an innate willingness and the ability to make you feel welcomed. Four Seasons claims the lowest employee turnover rate in the industry[1] and they have many great candidates for every open position. In other words, their culture is a magnate for the kind of people they want to attract. Wouldn't it be a luxury to have many great candidates for every open position? If your staff is remarkable, you are very likely exposing them to something they have never experienced. No matter what demographic you are recruiting from, it's a safe bet that your organization has never thought they were remarkable as a team. It

---

[1] Fortune Magazine, February 4, 2008

stands to reason that some of your people think they are exceptional, but every organization struggles with developing an identity that motivates the behavior of the masses. Your people will be amazed at the power they have to influence customer loyalty and a deep sense of pride will develop. Four Seasons does not have a frequent guest program and they charge top dollar for their rooms, but business people and vacationers alike look forward to their stay. The hotel chain credits its remarkable people as being the difference maker.

During a stay at a Four Seasons I encountered a housekeeper arriving at work at 5:00 a.m. We were in a remote hallway, no one was around and I was on my way to the health club. The woman stopped, put her bags down and asked me if I was enjoying my stay. No one was looking, but she was doing the right thing. She didn't do the right thing because she was being forced. I believe she did it because she enjoys making guests feel welcomed. If your entire workforce acted like that housekeeper, it's a safe bet someone will be referencing your business in a book in the near future too.

Building Your Program

Your training and transformation program should be tailored to suit your business. It's the best way to make sure it's meaningful, interesting and enduring. Most businesses want to launch a Hello Culture because they see it as a way to overwhelm their customers. More and more businesses, however, are now launching the program because they like the positive effect on their employees. The Hello Culture inspires your people to check their attitude in the workplace and serves as a reminder that it's good business to be outgoing and engaging. We've talked about the fact that the Hello Culture will become the center of your cultural identity so putting your current business culture into words is a great place to start. What would your employees say if you asked them what the culture is at your workplace? This is not a request for an eloquent outline. It's just a simple question to the average person in your business. If your people struggle to understand the question, or if they can only quote lines from some of your top level marketing materials, then you're on the scent of something really important. Every good organization has some type of cultural identity. What's yours? You don't need your people to all quote the same verse. In fact, you want people describing your culture in their own words around the same concept. The Hello Culture creates that center for you. The employee quotes that you'll get out of this are very inspirational. You really want your organization to be excited, energized and enthusiastic about your business. If your people sound flat, disengaged or uninspired, you'll find your journey into The Hello Culture to be very uplifting. Don't forget about the boss in the comic strip. You can't do this without being fully invested, but the good news is building a program is easy and being fully invested is fun. Let's get started.

Steps in building a program

Develop your strategy. Before leaving on vacation you have to know what will make you happy, what you can afford, how you're going to get there, and what you'll do to have fun. Building your Hello Culture strategy is similar to the vacation analogy. Let's start with the first, simple question. What will make you happy about implementing The Hello Culture? This question is worth a moment of reflection. If your culture lacks enthusiasm or inspiration you might be happy if you see your people start to move with a greater sense of purpose. Larger organizations tend to homogenize initiatives for the masses, which often sound great in business magazines, but fail to fully capture the focus of an employee's imagination. If that's you, then perhaps you're looking for a program that does not violate your corporate philosophy but gives your operation new-found spirit that will help your business performance. If your business and your people have the opportunity to regularly impress your customers, then you're right in the sweet spot for launching the Hello Culture. Your goal for your program is probably to help make your customers extremely loyal by making your people remarkable.

What can you afford to spend in launching your Hello Culture? There are countless examples of company programs that were well-funded, but fizzled because they lacked a clear focus or because business initiatives changed. Since we've all seen initiatives come up short in spite of resources, you shouldn't conclude your Hello Culture initiative will succeed or fail depending on how much you're willing to spend. Your success will be directly proportional to your commitment and your enthusiasm, not your investment. With all that said, you need to have some sense about investment. For organizations with staff greater than 500 people you should plan roughly a minimum of $50-$75 per person. These costs include things like the development of training programs, train the trainer programs, and your incentive awards. Since all organizations have different accounting philosophies, we have not included the cost of a staff member being away from their desk for 1 to 2 hours of training, the cost of using internal training rooms, and we have not added the cost of you and your manager's time to learn and train the classes. By the way, I strongly encourage you to get personally engaged in this. You will find it very uplifting. Smaller organizations are likely to incur costs of about 15%-20% more than the estimates above. It goes without saying your costs will ultimately be impacted by your own imagination. You could easily spend a lot less or a lot more, but you'll find that professional trainers will view this as a remarkably small investment versus the returns it will offer to your business.

Our vacation analogy now takes us to the question, "how will we get there?" I've alluded to the fact that your leadership team needs to be zealous in their commitment to this program. In other words, they're your vehicle that will get you to your destination. If you're the head of your business or the chief idea person then congratulations! You'll do great in getting this launched. Don't forget that all-important business axiom that says, "Everyone takes the cues from the top." Your management team needs to drink the Kool-Aid™. You'll need to kick-start things with that team. Since your management team is vital to your success, perhaps it's best to start them off by building some alignment around the state of affairs regarding employee attitude toward your customers. Better yet, what is your management's team attitude toward your customers? There are countless methods of getting to the root of this question. You can easily pick your own to suit your business, but the one I like the best starts with a simple question—"Why should our customers do business with us?" It's an ideal question because it focuses the team on your customer which should be the starting point for nearly every conversation in any industry. It is very likely that the answers you get from your team will focus in three areas: 1)your products and value they add to your customers, 2) the price of your products and 3) your people. You can pursue the discussions around product and price if you like, but I would quickly assess the importance of your people in your customer's decision to do business with you. It goes without saying that your people can move your customer's loyalty quotient.

How Important are Your People in the Decision-Making Process of Your Customer?

	Nordstrom	Walmart	Lexus	Your Company
Product				
Price				
People				
	100%	100%	100%	100%

It's easier to determine the importance of people in your customer's decision making process when you compare your organization to other companies. The average Walmart customer does not expect a Walmart associate to assist in buying decisions. People tend to place price as a big driver at Walmart mostly because that's an essential part of their marketing campaign. You can certainly go bottom-fishing at Lexus, but when you're looking for another $1,000 off the price of a $60,000 car you don't qualify as price sensitive. Lexus promotes superior products and unsurpassed service in their campaign. How important are your people in the buying decision of your customers?

Once your management team believes the people in your organization can inspire customer loyalty and that your employees are an important part of the buying decision, then you've built the alignment you need to get the management team bought into creating your Hello Culture. Management alignment is critical, but once you achieve that you'll need a bona fide campaign to teach your people and spread the message. This training program will not be difficult to build. You should think about a program that lasts between one and two hours. There are a few key messages that you'll need to incorporate:

- Define how important your people are in the buying decision of your customers
- Demonstrate the relevance of making customers feel welcomed and valued
- Highlight some attitudes and behaviors that can influence and repel people
- Outline the Hello journey, points of arrival and the destination
- Preview the steps you plan to take to make the Hello Culture real
- Deputize your staff and create personal accountability to take action

What will you do to have fun with your Hello Culture? It's a lot of fun to watch your employees take a lead role in making your customers happy. It's even more fun to let your customers tell your employees how impressed they are with your people. In a short amount of time you'll be able to promote your success in a number of areas. The first and best "fun zone" is to have your customers give live testimonials about their opinion of your staff. You get to feed everyone's ego by letting your customer stand up and talk about their experience. Asking a customer to address some of your staff in real time is an invitation to allow the customer to give back to your employees as a show of thanks for their treatment. Customers love it! You are creating a very tight connection between you and your customer when you ask them to speak to your employees. It's not a connection that will soon be lost or forgotten. Very few customers have ever been asked to speak to the employees of a service provider. It's almost guaranteed that your customer will leave the building feeling invigorated by having been invited to speak to your staff. Meanwhile your staff will be amazed at what they are hearing. There's also a very good chance that your customer will embellish their experience to sound masterful, which will also accrue greater value to your people. It's a real win-win. Genuine employee empowerment is another accomplishment that you should play with. Ask your employees how they feel about their role in winning new accounts, customers or clients. The more your people talk about their successes and their role in winning over customer the more you will ingrain the Hello Culture into the fabric of your organization. I would stay away from employee surveys and make this more of a mini town hall experience. There is nothing more powerful and empowering than to invite members of your staff to talk to one another about their experiences with customers.

Redefine Your Employees' Jobs

Here's an image: Your employee actually starts a conversation with your customer. If you work outside the retail industry the customer will likely ask your employee what they do in your business. What will the employee say? I am an agent. I'm a paralegal. I am an operator. I process claims. I work in customer service. Not only do answers like this miss the opportunity to help sell and differentiate your business, but they're also very boring and have the tendency to shut down the conversation. Those aren't answers to the question. Why not spice it up and let your employees act like rock stars also?

Customer: Hi Jena, it's nice to meet you. What do you do here?"
                Jena (paralegal): I helped a person avoid being taken off life support."

Jena (operator): "I make it easy for our customers to get fast answers."

Jena (claims):   "I help cancer patients focus on recovery."

Jena (customer service): "I help our military who are fighting overseas."

You have just made Jena much more remarkable in the eyes of the customer or the client. She has inspired the customer to engage her more deeply on the subject of her job. Chances are she will never mention her role in any mundane way again. It's pretty clear what we're doing here. We've coached the employee to tell a remarkable story about their job, rather than make a boring reference to their job title. It's an incredible conversation starter, and since the employee may not be adept at interpersonal communication, you've given the employee the chance to expound on a topic they know very well. You've also increased Jena's self-worth and her perceived value to the company by leaps and bounds. We achieve numerous things when we set the employee up with their own personal billboard, but the most significant is that Jena is now a dynamic advertisement for the valuable people that work in your organization. She is not a clerk or a number. She is part of the important fabric of your organization and she's doing work that is inspirational. Do you think the client would remember Jena better if she said she was a paralegal or if she said she helped represent a person that is now alert, vital and alive due to her actions? Imagine the impact if the client of a law firm knits together three such stories from people they meet before they meet with the partner?

Years ago in the early days of the NASA program a reporter approached a maintenance worker. The somewhat smug reporter asked the worker what he did there. The maintenance worker said, "I'm helping put a man on the moon." It's a well-told story in business, but it has remarkable alignment to this discussion. Your employees, like that maintenance worker, see themselves playing a role that aligns with your business mission and the business mission of the customer. There is no rule anywhere in any business book that says you have to answer with your job title when asked what you do. If you think about it, answering with a job title is silly and doesn't answer the question anyway. The billboard your employees wear about their role in your organization is one of the most powerful tools you can develop en route to building your Hello Culture. The image of your business in your customers' eyes will be positively influenced by the remarkable people with whom you work.

Prepare for Your
Customer's Visit . . . Everyday

Your business environment should be as welcoming as your people. This doesn't mean you have to go out and over spend on fashion and design. Bring a close friend into your office for the first time. Ask them what they think. Ask them what they see, what they notice, what they feel and what they smell. If your friend isn't noticing your business, your brand or your desired message when they walk in the door then you've just discovered the first thing you need to investigate. Since the manner in which your friend was greeted and serviced is the common thread throughout this book, we'll focus here on the message your business environment is sending. After all, your business environment needs to project a warm greeting also.

A big part of building, changing or influencing your culture is determined by your workspace. It's a lot like selling your house. Prior to putting your house on the market, you always knock out a "to do" list, followed by some major organizing, then you wrap it up with a good cleaning. If you're really interested in making your customer feel welcome, why not follow your realtor's advice? Your lobby or your reception area makes the first impression on your guests. First and foremost your reception area really needs to be up-to-date. If you're promoting bygone campaigns, old marketing images, bad plants or tired looking wall art, then you're sending a signal that your business is in decline. It's a little bit like leaving junk in the front yard of your house. Realtors call it curb appeal and when your lobby area is in a declining state you send the message that you really don't care what people think anymore. I was recently sitting in a doctor's office and reading a story in a popular business magazine. I had long suspected that my home subscription delivery time was unreliable and reading this article that interested me confirmed my suspicion. Once I saw that the magazine I was reading was actually 14 months old my perspective changed. This doctor, who makes the patients wait for nearly 60 minutes, has a perspective that a patient will read anything in order to help kill the insufferable queue time. That doctor compounds his problem because his waiting room provides seating for roughly a 30 minute wait. At about 40 minutes into your wait your guilty conscience makes you sacrifice your seat for the people toting oxygen or walking with a cane. I really think he's just one step away from giving out the vibrating pagers made popular at IHOP or The Cheesecake Factory, because I was finally tracked down standing in the hallway outside his open door. Medical professionals can say whatever they want about the pressure to see patients, but this story is all too common and it leaves patients very vulnerable to changing providers. For the rest of us we just need to be aware of what our lobby says to our customers or clients.

Now that your customer has come inside your business, what does your work environment say to them? If you want to look like an orderly, efficient, welcoming business, you really need to discourage your staff from having whacky signs or piles of paper on their desk. The same is true for outdated award and recognition programs. An employee of the month award from 4 years ago is not going to do much to make your customer feel great about the current level of service they are receiving. The important point to take away is that if you're not paying attention to the way your business looks and the messages it's sending, then you're sending a message that is not very welcoming.

The appearance of your work environment also helps build the culture of your business. There is really no excuse for an office environment in a service business to look like a mess. If your employee population takes pride in their "neighborhood" they will take more pride in their job. Let's go back to the real estate analogy for a moment. Neighborhoods that are in disrepair bring lower values and exclude many people who want to and can afford to live elsewhere. The same is true for prospective great employees and impressionable customers. The examination room at my doctor's office is a Greenfield for observing quirky things. Someone in the practice has decided to store medical and office supplies in shipping boxes inside the room near the door. A hand-written sign in Spanish was slapped on one of his trash cans and various tattered notices to patients were taped to his wall. I'm pretty sure he wouldn't do the same in his home near his front door. So why do we let our business environment become a distraction? I know what his examination room would look without all that stuff because I talked to him about it when he came in. He made two of the changes right away. He loved it and he appreciated the difference.

Great employees want to work in environment that has competitive pay, offers advancement and places value in its staff. The drive-by effect from a messy office is very powerful. Of course, this changes by industry so you'll have to make your own determination about what constitutes a good look. An advertising agency will clearly want a different look from a call center. Your customers take cues from your environment, so it's a good idea to make it accrue in your favor. Lastly, your existing employee population needs to know that you take your workplace appearance very seriously. The type of employees that you really want to retain will embrace this cultural norm.

There is actually some significant science around challenging employees to maintain your workplace appearance. There is a program derived from the popular Six Sigma and Lean programs called 5S. The basic principle is that businesses run more efficiently and effectively if everything is kept in its proper place—not to mention the fact that the business looks much better. The 5 Ss stand for: sort, straighten, sweep, standardize and self-discipline. You can read up on the 5S program elsewhere, but a central theme to the 5S program is most relevant for this book. A foundational principle in 5S is, "if the work team can't even keep the workplace in order, then what does is it say about our ability execute on serious improvements to our business?" In other words, 5S is the ante to get in the game and it may be a good indicator of how willing your organization is to creating a Hello environment. Have you ever been reluctant to let a guest in your house wander aimlessly, or have you been reduced to apologizing for the mess? In either case you feel that way because you are not proud of the way things look. Customers and employees alike sense the same things in the work place. We all want to be proud of our environment, so why not let your business environment be a source of pride for your workforce?

Why Aren't They Doing It?

Earlier I mentioned that you might see employees refusing to take any initiative at first. In fact, you'll see employees go out of their way to avoid a customer interaction. I've talked about employee reluctance to make the effort to say hello to a customer. There are really four primary reasons why an employee will avoid a customer encounter: they don't like their job, they are shy, they are having a truly bad day or because saying hello is antithetical to their personality. The greatest of these is the fact that saying hello is outside the comfort zone of many people. If you wander through life not saying hello to people, then being asked to start doing it is uncomfortable. In order to say hello to someone you actually have to notice them. To notice someone you have to walk with your head up and your eyes focused on people coming at you. Conduct your own study on this tomorrow. Watch how many people are purposely looking away or preoccupied as you try to make eye contact with them. Now it becomes much easier to see why customers are ignored. If you transport all those people into your workplace, you can begin to appreciate the challenge. Making the Hello Culture real in your business is not as simple as just issuing a memo.

You really need to get people to understand the personal and professional value of breaking out of their comfort zone. I often ask audiences to choose from a list of things that might be outside their comfort zone. The list of sixteen includes things like going to a different gas station, trying a new church or turning off the television for 3 days. Once everyone has chosen something I ask how many people are actually going to try what they said they would try. Without fail about 50% of the people raise their hands, meaning that 50% of the audience has already given up. Committing to do something uncomfortable and then actually doing it is tough. Don't underestimate how difficult it is for most people to say hello to people. Like anything in life, people need to get comfortable with something before they feel okay about it. I make light of my own insecurities. I often tell a story about visiting an employee in the hospital. I tell everyone that I came up with 10 reasons not to go before I realized I was just avoiding a difficult situation that made me uncomfortable. The purpose of the story is not about going to the hospital. Because I talked myself into doing something that I was uncomfortable with, I actually discovered a store, a university and the city zoo. I would never have seen or discovered all three had it not been for me breaking through my comfort zone.

It's really important for employees to know that you know it's not simple. They need to see that challenging their comfort zone with something as simple as saying hello can yield remarkable results. There is a great sociological phenomenon associated with this. When people take the initiative to say hello, they are the first to speak. It demonstrates self-confidence and it opens the door to communication. It's a subtle way to play offense while, at the same time, showing yourself as very welcoming and approachable. No matter how many examples you provide, people will only adopt it when they are ready. You can't force it, but you and your workforce can spirit the slow adopters along by just doing what is natural for you.

Make Your Customers Easy to Spot

The retail, restaurant and medical industry makes it pretty easy for customers to be identified. If you're not wearing some version of a uniform, then you're probably a customer. Very few service businesses wear company uniforms so how can you be sure that your employees will be able to spot a customer when they see one coming? Remember that the goal here is to give your employees an advantage so that they know a customer is coming their way or that there is a customer waiting in your lobby.

The best way to make your customer feel welcome is to give them the keys to the city. It's really very simple. Customers should never wear the same visitor badge that is reserved for a visiting technician, an off-site employee or a candidate. They need to wear a badge that is distinctive and easy to spot from a distance. They should wear one that is reserved exclusively for customers. If you're giving customers peel and stick badges, then it's time you look into an upgrade. The best one I've seen is a simple gold badge with your company logo worn with a lanyard around their neck. Even the lanyard color should be exclusive to customer badges. Once you do this you're giving every one of your employees a key advantage in the art of welcoming your customers. This strategy ties in nicely with something we talked about at the beginning. Let's set a goal of having your customer take a self-guided tour of your facility. With a gold badge in plain view and a fully engaged workforce, your business is poised to execute one of the most memorable events in business history. Wearing the gold badge creates the effect like those magical staircases in Harry Potter. Every turn your customer takes will result in another natural segue into the most amazing business culture in your industry. It's fun to imagine all the small and large celebrations that will make your customer feel welcomed, appreciated and valued. There is probably very little else they will want to talk about when you finally fetch them from your staff.

You need to take the initiative to make sure all your employees know when a customer is coming to visit your business. It gives your people a heads up and it reinforces all the behaviors you expect them to exhibit. You should tell your employees as much about the people and the business that is coming to visit you as possible. They should know the easy things like business name, location, customer size and who is coming. Keep in mind that the more your staff knows, the more equipped they will be to make an overwhelming impression upon your customer. Make sure your staff knows who within your company owns the relationship with the customer. It's very powerful for your office-based staff to help support the efforts of your sales or relationship team. It creates greater continuity within your organization and the customer will see it. Find out from your sales team anything you can about your guests. I like to know where they went to school or something about their family life. If you're really on your game you can place mementos around your building or conference room that reminds your customer of home. American Airlines ran a marketing campaign built around this concept a few years ago. It featured a weary business traveler who was on a long international trip. When the traveler arrived at the airport for his trip home the agent asked if there was anything she could do for him. He smiled and looked at the American Airlines plane at the gate. The powerful image of a plane that reminded him of home was quite comforting to him.

The same can be true for customers that travel to see you. Make them feel at home in your home. They will notice it. All of this accrues in your favor and helps assure your customers will be overwhelmed by the reception they received when visiting you.

Make Your Employees Easy to Talk to

We see another important aspect of The Hello Culture every day, but you probably fail to stop and think about the potential value it has to your business. Name-tags. We see name-tags everywhere, but most of us think they are reserved for consumer businesses, conferences and technicians with their name embroidered on their shirt. When we go to conferences or training programs we all suit up with a name-tag. We do it because it opens the lines of communication between two people. If you really want your employees and your customers to open up to each other then make your employees more approachable. The name-tag serves as an invitation for your guest to speak to your staff.

The immediate response by a service business whose employees do not currently wear name-tags will be negative. It's automatic. It's the same response people had when they were told they should start wearing seat belts when driving. Of course, that paradigm shifted and so will this one. You can have a lot of fun with name-tags so don't be so quick to dismiss this idea. How do you think a front-line employee would feel if they had a name-tag that identified them as being terrific? If you really want to reward your top performers, why not let them proudly wear their accomplishments in plain sight for everyone to see? These are just a couple ideas, but you are only limited by your imagination.

Technology developments have now made it much easier to convert all your employees to name-tags. Most businesses these days have an identification badge system for security purposes. Since employees' names on badges are typically printed in a small font they serve little, if any, value in helping to visually identify someone by name. Add to that the fact that many badges are worn at waist level and you have an identification badge that is really only good for security inspections or swipes at the card reader. What if the security badge doubled as a name-tag? It's quite simple these days thanks to RFID (radio frequency identification device) chips. An RFID chip sends a radio signal that is picked up by receivers. No longer will your staff have to swipe their badge and the technology allows security to immediately know the location of an employee while on-site. With RFID technology you can now turn an ID badge into a bona fide name-tag that promotes your company, your employee's name and your employee's accomplishments. There are many types of badges in the marketplace, but the one that will work the best for the majority of employees is one that has a magnetic bar. A magnetic bar will not destroy clothes and it tends to stay in full view better than more traditional pin tags.

Win More Great Candidates

Once your employees are deputized and equipped to say hello to all your customers you'll begin to see some of the collateral benefits of The Hello Culture. Your employees will begin zeroing in on candidates and job applicants. Being a candidate is like living in a glass house. Perhaps you've forgotten how unsettling it is to be a candidate. These days, candidates show up in their best dressed outfit but your workforce is walking around in business casual. Candidates are easy to spot, which adds to their anxiety and nervousness. Let's assume for a moment that the candidate in your lobby is outstanding and the person will have competing offers. If your employees approach the candidate, welcome him or her and spend a minute talking about life at your company, your chances of winning the candidate will go up. We've all heard about how colleges recruit great athletes. If we overlaid the business world with college recruiting, the recruit would come to campus and meet with the coach and the admissions director only. Athletic programs don't do that. Long ago they learned that it's best to let the recruit learn about the university through another athlete. Why don't we do that in business? You really don't need to go as far as sending all your candidates out for lunch with employees, but why not have your employees welcome candidates to your business?

In The Hello Culture there is not a series of planned actions. Once your employees develop a desire to welcome people to your business it will happen anyway. In an effort to give your employees a leg up you should really develop a separate badge for candidates. The same principle holds here as it does for your customers. Your candidate will be squired around your building from interview to interview. If the candidate is wearing a badge that is easy to spot, your employees will carry the day. The impact on a candidate will be profound as he or she is approached and welcomed by employee after employee. It is a huge selling advantage that will make a terrific impression on your candidate. The other thing you're accomplishing while welcoming your candidate is that you are training your future new employee in the art of The Hello Culture.

There's a good chance that your training program could be delivered online in a 10 minute segment if the candidate experienced it first-hand and then sees it put into practice once they join the organization. At this point in your history you have achieved what you set out to do. You have developed a cultural norm that regenerates itself every day. Your employees have achieved an unconscious competence for this behavior and your business will thrive as a result. Now you just have to be ready to handle the throng of journalists and television shows that want to highlight your business for its remarkable people.

Reinforce Your Hello Culture

The best way to create a new culture is to reinforce positive behaviors. Just like the boss in the cartoon strip you will not be able to simply will this to happen. You and your leadership team will absolutely have to model every behavior of The Hello Culture, but in addition to that you have to celebrate all the small victories along the way. You need to make time and resources available to get your Hello Culture launched.

After your training program is started you will need to nudge many of your employees to take action. Keep something important in mind. Many of your staff will be hesitant because they are either introverted, generally cranky or they still have not bought in. You already know who will grab this and run with it so you need to give them and others plenty of positive reinforcement as they pull the others along. Opening the lines of communication is the cheapest and best way to promote your Hello Culture. Your customers will start giving you headlines for your internal communications. Use them to your advantage. There is no reason to wait to start promoting what your customers are saying about your remarkable people when they leave your building.

Spend a few dollars on your program too. Why not give away some gift certificates and buy your people a sandwich for a job well done? You could use Starbucks, Subway or Blockbuster cards, all of which are always appreciated. You can administer your program whatever way you wish, but I prefer to implement a program that actually challenges specific employees to take some type of welcoming action. I think there is great value to linking specific actions with rewards. My recommendation is that you develop a program that invites your employee to create some type of welcoming experience or challenges them to do something unexpected. I would actually do both simultaneously, but we'll talk more about that in a minute. Why not hand out a special card that invites the employee to create some type of welcoming experience? Write the employee's name on the card with an expiration date. The program is simple in design, but powerful in action. The program has no rules and there is no verification necessary. The employee only has to do two things to earn their reward—they have to do something that is welcoming and then they have to come tell you or your senior managers what they did. Don't let the employees email or call you. You can figure out the logistics if you're multi-site operation or if you're the CEO so I am not evaluating every permutation for that reason. You want to use the moment as a way to connect with your employee, say thank you and hear what they did. Never say no and never challenge the story. Don't be worried about someone gaming the system because peer pressure will work wonders here. Early on you'll hear employees ask if what they did was okay or not, but in a short time they will have the program figured out. The program takes on a life of its own because employees seek to one up other employees. You should fully expect that customers will start being greeted in your lobby, receive homemade cookies and hear large rounds of applause as time goes on. The actions of your employees will be great content for your internal communications and sales materials. You should even take license to present greater rewards for actions above and beyond. You should think about monthly or quarterly rewards for meritorious actions. You can also implement a complementary program that challenges an employee to do something unexpected. This program is designed to help hyper-charge your employees to take action outside their job scope. It also gives them a chance to do something for each other, for their manager, for a customer or for your business. The structure is the same so the employees need to come and talk to you about what it was they did.

It's no secret or great science what you're doing when you challenge people to take action and then reward them for a job well done. You're inviting people to act on stage with you. It may be uncomfortable for a variety of reasons, but you have to be resolute in your vision in order to turn them toward the future. I recommend you keep up with your challenge cards for at least two years. You may need less time but I think the behavior will be fairly self-sustaining after that time. The most powerful thing you're doing when implementing a program like this is the handshake and the thank you. It puts you closer to your employees and it keeps you personally invested in The Hello Culture.

Final Thoughts

Your workforce will be a very different, formidable team when you achieve the goals you set for your Hello Culture. Your employees will seek out your customers when they are in your business. You need to reinforce to your employees that it's okay to go up to a customer when they are touring your business to welcome and engage them. Your employees should be empowered to approach a customer anytime they are in open areas of your business. In other words, unless the customer or client is in a conference room they are fair game. The employees can interrupt a tour or a discussion in an effort to say hello and welcome. If the customer wants and needs privacy you can always take them to a conference room. Don't forget, you want your customers to feel like rock stars and you want your employees to be fully engaged in your selling process.

Be patient with your organization as it evolves. It's really easy to assume that your entire organization will jump into action since you're only asking them to say hello. You'll have to train, coach, reinforce and reward positive behaviors over and over to achieve your goals. Along the way you will see more and more flashes of people stepping up. It's very powerful for an employee to see themselves as playing a key role in selling and retaining customers. You will tap into a sense of pride to which most employees have never been exposed. Beyond pride comes empowerment. Beyond empowerment comes your new cultural identity. When your workforce takes full ownership of customer selling and retention they will be faithfully engaged in your top line. This is not a phenomenon that the majority of businesses can achieve. You will have differentiated yourself in your industry and you will be a model for other businesses to follow.

Isn't it remarkable that it all stems from something we have all known for a very long time? It's nice to make people feel welcomed. Everyone in the equation feels good about making people feel good.

Good luck and remember to say "hello" to the next person you see.

www.ingramcontent.com/pod-product-compliance
Lightning Source LLC
Chambersburg PA
CBHW021935170526
45157CB00005B/2320